Alarum Within

For Linda,
Thank you for supporting the arts in Red Deer!
Enjoy

Alarum Within

theatre poems

Kimmy Beach

Affairs of the Arts 2005

TURNSTONE PRESS

Turnstone Press
607-100 Arthur Street
Artspace Building
Winnipeg, MB
R3B 1H3 Canada
www.TurnstonePress.com

Turnstone Press gratefully acknowledges the assistance of The Canada Council for the Arts, the Manitoba Arts Council, the Government of Canada through the Book Publishing Industry Development Program and the Government of Manitoba through the Department of Culture, Heritage and Tourism, Arts Branch, for our publishing activities. The author wishes to acknowledge the assistance of the Alberta Foundation for the Arts.

The Canada Council | Le Conseil des Arts
for the Arts | du Canada

MANITOBA arts COUNCIL
CONSEIL DES DU MANITOBA

COMMITTED TO THE DEVELOPMENT OF CULTURE AND THE ARTS

The Alberta Foundation for the Arts

Alberta

Canada

Cover design: Tétro Design
Interior design: Sharon Caseburg
Printed and bound in Canada byKromar Printing Ltd. for Turnstone Press.

National Library of Canada Cataloguing in Publication Data

Beach, Kimmy, 1964-

  Alarum within : theatre poems / Kimmy Beach.
  ISBN 0-88801-279-9

  1. Theater—Poetry. I. Title.

PS8553.E119A77 2003   C811'.6   C2003-910336-6

PR9199.4.B43A77 2003

for Dawn Andrea Beach
1978-1998

Contents

Acknowledgements

Alarum Within

I.

WANTED! ACTORS!

Alarum Within

Time: Then.
Scene: A Woman. A Theatre. Dark.
Curtains. Whispers. Actors. Light.

Dramatis Personae:

A MURDERER
LADY MACBETH, Wife to
    Macbeth
OLIVER TWIST, an Orphan Boy
MOTHER COURAGE, an Old
    Woman pulling a Wagon
MR. DRESSUP, an Entertainer of
    Children
JESUS CHRIST, a Saviour
THREE NIECES
A DIRECTOR
COLIN and ALAN, two Actors
A NURSE
SEVERAL DEAD SOLDIERS, on a
    Battlefield
KAREN, Sister to the Stage
    Manager
SUSAN'S MOM, a Suicide
STU, an Actor, later Husband
    to the Stage Manager
A FAMOUS HYPNOTIST
JUDAS ISCARIOT, Betrayer of
    Jesus Christ
A PHARMACIST
A STAGE MANAGER
ROBIN, an Actor portraying
    Jesus Christ
A COLLECTOR
A WOUNDED SOLDIER
LARRY, Brother to the Stage
    Manager

THREE WEYARD SISTERS
JERRY, the Commissionaire
FINNEGAN, a Puppet in shape
    of a Dog
A DESIGNER
MOM, Mother to the Stage
    Manager
A SICK WOMAN, in a Bed,
    Feverish
BILL SIKES, another Murderer
FAGAN, a Desperate Pickpocket
FRANK, an Actor
APPARITIONS OF THREE
    CHILDREN, Dead
A LITTLE GIRL who loves
    Mr. Dressup
A FAMOUS ACTOR portraying
    Jesus Christ
DAWN, niece to the Stage Manager
A VISITING DIRECTOR
JULIAN OF NORWICH, a Mystic
CASEY, a Puppet in shape of a Boy
RYAN, an Actor
A DOCTOR
HILDEGARD OF BINGEN,
    a Mystic
MACBETH, Thane of Glamis,
    Thane of Cawdor, and
    King hereafter
SEVERAL ACTORS, unnamed
AN AUDIENCE

5

WANTED! ACTORS!

Actor /·ækt3r/ n. a moving, semi-permeable membrane of flesh-toned reflective surfaces. Used primarily to give perspective to furniture size and colour. Often fitted with garments to further complement the furniture and other surroundings. Genus: Waiterus Reflecticus★

WANTED! ACTORS!
Collector will pay top dime for a dozen actors for use in medical and behavioural experiments. Must be easily replaceable at any *Actor Store* if accidentally dropped or killed. Must have discernible talent. Must not be whiny or allergic to make-up, floorboards, fog machines, fellow actors, wigs, costumes, fabric or dogs. Must be able to find a light and hold a prop without hurting themselves.

SPECIFICATIONS FOR FEMALES
No dazed looks or crying fits. Must not think she is Lady Macbeth an hour before curtain. Those sporting *can't talk, in character* façades not welcome. Should be willing to wear corsets without complaining about diaphragm constriction.

SPECIFICATIONS FOR MALES
Must be marginally intelligent, fiercely devoted, and fairly handsome. Must be able to find his scabbard without stabbing himself in the leg. Should not ask questions such as: *Why is he always cutting my lines?*

★ source unknown

HOUSING DETAILS

Collector has arranged semi-private natural habitat. Scripts are strewn about with various offers of desirable roles (Lady Macbeth, Jesus of Nazareth, etc), authentic stage lighting, fetching costumes, and simulated audience complete with applause/laugh track. Actors will be free to perform with no appreciable change in lifestyle. Breeding carefully monitored.

Please include photo, shoe size and all notable shortcomings (swollen ego, fondness for random and annoying quotations from Shakespeare, susceptibility to every germ within city limits, inflated sense of acting/singing/dancing ability, etc).

Reply to: Box 2850,
Red Deer, Alberta

Q to Q

[A Play in One Act]

Dramatis Personae:
> The Stage Manager
> Donny, Lights and Sound
> Greg, Technical Director
> Frank, an actor

[Friday, 6:45 pm. Work lights. The Stage Manager enters through the upstage right door carrying a Coke and a prompt script. The latch is taped. The door closes silently behind her. Donny has flown in the first LX and is downstage checking the C-clamps on the instruments. Greg is tightening the caster brakes on the upstage right platform. From the booth, we hear David Wilcox's *Greatest Hits:* "Downtown Came Uptown for You." An actor at the back of the house paces from house right to left reciting lines: *Do you not hope your children shall be Kings, / When those that gave the Thane of Cawdor to me, / Promis'd no less to them.*]

STAGE MANAGER [From the downstage edge]: Frank—out! We have a lot of work to do. Besides, I don't know how you can do your lines over David Wilcox.

FRANK: I wish they'd shut that shit off. I'm trying to get the feel of the space.

STAGE MANAGER: This is tech time, Frank. Out!

DAVID WILCOX: . . . *downtown came uptown for you.*

FRANK [Grumbling]: All right. Christ. [Exits through the house right doors into the lobby.]

STAGE MANAGER: How's it going, guys?

DONNY: Good. I just have to focus the 'Banquo's ghost' spot and you can start.

8

STAGE MANAGER: Thanks. Greg, what the hell is up with those wheels? I'll rip them off myself if they don't start working properly. And why isn't the floor cloth done? I've got a full run-through in the morning.

GREG: I don't know—ask the designer. [Pause.] I'll see what I can do. Just let me get these brakes taken care of, and you can go ahead.

DAVID WILCOX: *Downtown came uptown for you.*

STAGE MANAGER: Thank you, gentlemen. All right, let's get this over with before midnight strikes, shall we? Everybody grab a coffee. We'll start the Q to Q run-through in ten. [To the booth]: Could somebody up there turn off Wilcox? The call is ten minutes.

One Flew over the Cuckoo's Nest 1985
[for Stu]

how easy it was for you
run on stage at top speed,
shriek your lines
pretend to hallucinate
deal cards that weren't there
one to me one to you

always in character an hour
before rehearsal running through
the basement passages wide
eyed and panting in nut-house issue
beige and too tight khakis

it was up to you, McMurtry, and the
others to move the chairs into
a circle for the group therapy scenes
then put them back around
the common room tables afterward
Nurse Ratchet was not required
to help but often did
you could never remember where
the god damn things went

rehearsal began with you
tripping on a fold-up
chair and throwing it across the stage
what the hell is THIS?
had to be my fault
three inches off its spikes
it threw you out of character
when you stubbed your
ego on it

give you actors a prop, I always said
and you'll manage to hurt yourselves
you could hurt yourselves with balloons
and marshmallows and
find a way to blame
the stage manager

I watched you fume
asshole I thought
and knew I loved you

The Wells Fargo Wagon

[*The Music Man* 1986]

they stand in *finale* position
arms outstretched   big jazz hands
they smile into the front-of-house lights
hit that final chorus

two dogs, fourteen children
the entire Red Deer Royals Marching Band
and the Wells Fargo Wagon
fire engine red and wooden with
white letters a foot high
trimmed in gold paint
pulled by a jittery white horse
on loan from a rancher
out west of Rimbey

if that horse shits on my stage
I tell The Director
you're cleaning it up

on opening night, the lights
the wild applause throw that poor horse
into madness
he leaves a steaming pile between himself
and the wagon full of shiny
trumpets and French horns Professor Hill
ordered for the *Minuet in G*

the actors plunge
forward with the Act One closing number
crisscrossing, high stepping
stage left to stage right
hats tilted, skirts
and petticoats lifted
in perfect choreography
singing for all they're worth

the show must go on
shit underfoot or not

here's the scene at intermission:
The Director—in full view
of the nicely coiffed audience
members who choose to stay
in their seats to watch the scene
change—in his tuxedo, dung on his
perfect black shoes, carrying
sawdust and a shovel makes all this
horse shit worthwhile

Dancemania 1986!
with Miss Wendy and the Advanced Tap Class

Julie runs toward me
just as fast as her pink
tapdancer legs will carry her
cream chiffon swishes back
and forth on her seventeen
-year-old tapdancer butt
batons wave in the blue-tinted
darkness backstage
Kimmy, have you seen my shoes?

Have you checked your feet?
and there they are!
she clacks happily on
to tap her little brains out

and the audience thinks
the magic happens *on* stage

The Man They Call . . .

he's a good three hundred pounds
you'd think he could hypnotize himself
into dropping some weight

the audience roars on stage
dancing   stamping like horses
they think it's hot and
begin to remove clothing
shoes, baseball hats, a T-shirt
reveals a tiger
stripe bra, a lifted toupée
shows a balding head

he stops them before it becomes
indecent   their fifteen
seconds of fame
over too soon
they won't remember

I'm the assistant stage manager
two performances of The Greatest
Hypnotist In The World
I pull the curtain
as if I were revealing
The Three-Legged Dog
-Faced Boy to jaded carnival goers
cue the house lights
replenish his water glass

his son runs the sound board
stage right   (he adjusts the level of his
dad's mic and the one held by the first-year
Psych student who thinks he's Elvis caught
in a swarm of bees)
unhurried   the son so calm he could be
setting the table
a mic fades for a moment
the audience doesn't notice
they're laughing so hard

stage right the boy waits for his next cue
his father tromps off stage flailing
panting *what the hell is the matter with you?*
can't you keep one god damn microphone on,
you little shit? Jesus Christ!

the boy sits as though hypnotized
sets microphone levels for the next young
woman who will be told she is Tina Turner
with an unbearably itchy
shoulder blade

he is red   panting   his face
contorted with the effort it takes
to resist hitting the boy where I
would see him do it
at the edge of the wings he stops
breathes   smiles   puffs up
walks on to applause
arms held wide
The Funniest
Live Show You Will Ever See

Black-Edged Telegram Poem

[*Late-Nite Cabaret* 1986]

the manual reads: *Should a*
black-edged telegram arrive,
the Stage Manager shall hold it
until after
curtain call.

~

she smiles   it's fixed on
thick make-up
blending around her eyes
the flowered costume snug
on her thin frame

let's get out there   she laughs   *good show*
everybody!
on the way to the stage
without looking up she passes me
a slip of pink paper
thick with commissionaire scrawl

I see her in profile, dusty air through
an arc of Trudy Blue spilling on her
upturned face
she snaps her fingers
to the music from the three-piece
combo in the corner
sings the first lines of
Moondance

Susan. A call came
for you. Your mother
killed herself.
9:42 pm Saturday.
From Jerry. P.S.
Sorry.

II.
Mr. Dressup

Dear Friend

[for Ernie Coombs]

If you write to us, said Mr. Dressup
one morning in late 1969,
I'll write back to you.
I watched Casey tuck
Finnegan into the tree house bed
breathless I waited for them to say
goodbye to me then ran to mom

she wrote feverishly for her child possessed
> *mom say dear Mr. Dressup and say I*
> *love Casey and mom say*
> *I want to live in a tree house too and say I always*
> *put the lid back on the glue and say*
> *I wish I was Casey because you love Casey*
> *and say why doesn't Finnegan ever bark and say*

six weeks later I held a postcard
bearing the largest rubber stamp
impression I have ever seen
> *Dear Friend*   (I told my mom
> my name's not Friend) *Thank you*
> *very much for your letter.*
> *From Casey, Finnegan, and me,*
> *Mr. Dressup.*

the full text all on one stamp

twenty-five years later he is in town
I am the stage manager
for Casey and Finnegan's farewell tour
Even a five-year-old knows a
stamp when she sees one
I tell him shaky   a quarter century
needing to say it

ten minutes later I hold a postcard
with a picture of the three of them

Dear Kimmy,
Thank you for your letter.
Sorry it took me so long to answer.

Love,
Mr. Dressup

Raiders of the Lost Tickle Trunk

it sits at centre stage waiting
for the two-thirty show
deep orange with a rounded top
yellow and blue stars flowers
moons painted on all sides
two shiny handles
a gold clasp on the front

I sit in the wings stage right
my hands nervous in my lap
waiting for the sound check
Mr. Dressup's footsteps echo in the long
stairwell from dressing room to stage
I stand to greet him, smooth my
backstage blacks, clear my throat
he opens the door

I try to ask without sounding
like a lovesick child
Of course you can look inside, Kim
he says, *but I'm afraid*
you might be disappointed

Impossible!
I know what's inside
Mr. Dressup's Tickle Trunk
magic costumes that could turn
him into a lion one moment (but never
a scary one) and a mouse the next
a magic wand, piles of coloured fabric and hats
noses, whiskers and glasses of all kinds
Casey's gender identity
Finnegan's secret voice

now and then to prove he was magic
he would pull out something
larger than the trunk itself
a ten foot ladder, for instance
or a pair of stilts

he doesn't swirl his hand over it
the way he does on TV
he simply bends and lifts the lid
stands back   *there you go*
I lean over carefully   (I know your
face melts off if you stand too close
I watched it happen to those fools in
Raiders of the Lost Ark who
thought they could open the
Ark of the Covenant and not die)
inside   a green felt Robin Hood hat
two plastic flutes   one black magic marker
some sawdust   the most
devastating sawdust in the world

And Me, Mr. Dressup

[A Play in One Act]

Dramatis Personae:
> Mr. Dressup
> A Little Girl

[A sound stage, CBC Television, 10 November 1969. Mr. Dressup is cleaning up construction paper and glue from the previous taping. A colourful vest with all manner of fasteners is draped over a blue make-up chair in the corner. A little girl enters. She is dressed in black and carries a clipboard. She has a pencil behind her ear and a stopwatch on a rope around her neck.]

LITTLE GIRL: Fifteen minutes, Mr. Coombs. Can I get you a drink? Coffee or something?

MR. DRESSUP: Call me Ernie. [He finishes cleaning up and lays his cape and pirate hat in the Tickle Trunk.] I'm fine, thanks. Though Scotch straight up would be great. These three-show days are murder. [They both laugh.] Anything else?

LITTLE GIRL: Yeah. Why were you never there for me?

MR. DRESSUP [Sitting in the make-up chair and exhaling loudly]: God, I'm sick of hearing that. I'm not your father. I'm not responsible for you. I did not promise to *be there* for you.

LITTLE GIRL [She sits on the Tickle Trunk, her back hunched.]: I always imagined you loved me, but when it came right down to it, you weren't there. I wasn't important to you. You didn't even know me.

[A lighting technician crosses downstage carrying two instruments.]

MR. DRESSUP: You're right, I didn't know you, but I imagined you.

LITTLE GIRL: That's not good enough.

MR. DRESSUP [Exasperated, he slaps his palms against his legs and stands. He begins to pace.]: Well, Christ, what would be good enough?

LITTLE GIRL: I need a commitment.

MR. DRESSUP: What kind of commitment? [Pause.] Oh. I see. [He understands, walks to the little girl, picks up the strings attached to her shoulders and wrists and traces them back to the wooden sticks trailing behind her. He holds the sticks high over the little girl's head and lifts her from her seated position. The little girl goes through a series of dance movements and mime. He walks her to the Mr. Dressup set. The next taping begins.]

MR. DRESSUP [To the camera]: Hi boys and girls. Thank you for coming to visit us today. I'd like you to meet my new friend. She says I wasn't there for her when she was little, so now I'm making it up to her. [Mr. Dressup manipulates the strings attached to the little girl's hands so that she is pulling construction paper, scissors, magic markers and a glue stick out of the craft drawer.] Now, we'll do a special craft for a special little girl. [The two freeze in tableau. The audience understands that they are frozen forever. Lights. Curtain.]

I love the hands of this Old woman

I lie asleep in the orange trunk
my dog Finnegan lies next to me
he hears the lid open and
barks without making a sound
sometimes he bites my hair

his red felt tongue is glued
to the bottom of his mouth
he's not a real dog
real dogs need to pant to keep cool

I am lifted   she knows
I can't hold my own head up
opens the space at the bottom of my body
(perhaps I had legs once   I don't remember)
she slides her right hand cool
and wrinkled into me
slips her little finger into my right arm
her thumb in my left
her three fingers squeeze
into the straw and paper
that form my head
the tiny ring on her pinky
rubs my right shoulder

she slides her left hand into
my dog's rumpled body
her thumb fills his lower jaw
her four fingers in his nose
I often wonder why
he was given a mouth
and yet no sound
and me with so much to say

I love the hands of this old woman
she does all the talking for me
I don't mind
I am alive   awake

sometimes Mr. Dressup will pet Finnegan
or scratch him behind his ears
but I know it's me he loves

III.
Encephalitis

Hey Linda —

Think of this as a late Christmas or early birthday gift. It was written by a friend of ours – Stage Manager for years, English teacher, poet. All round cool lady.

Hope you are well.

Love,

Glynis

Encephalitis

[*Mother Courage* 1989]

i

Lighting the Wagon

we have fifty-one light cues
to write before tomorrow night's
run-through   no walkers
no one to stand still on stage
quiet, face to the lights
to mark key positions
for lighting the actors and props
I bring ripple chips
Gord brings *sake*
it's three in the morning

a wagon at centre stage
monstrous, fragile
clunky with old pots, tankards
creaky with bits of cloth and tea
I don't feel all that great

Mother Courage's worldly possessions
hauled through the Thirty Years War
I fade at four
Gord pours me another drink
we're almost done, baby

he flags dimmers up and down
blends Surprise Pink   Azure Blue
pools appear and disappear
at stage left as his index fingers play
the dimmers, slide on the light board
metal gobos splash the pattern of leaves
over bare wood
the wagon dances in my field of vision

I am hauling it in an endless circle
at centre stage circa 1624
key lights flicker in all corners
        my head
gelled with Burnt Umber

ii

Dress Rehearsal
[February 28]

I wake at eight, kiss Stu goodbye
he leaves for the barber shop
I stand and fall repeatedly
have to get to work
     fall
pissed off   *keep falling down the stairs and I'll*
be late   I am wearing
four T-shirts, no coat

I am so sick I don't know
I'm sick   I have to
get to work but I
can't see
colour and light obscure
the path to my door
I have to get to work
and rise from the kitchen
floor where I've fallen
leave the house with no
coat no keys no shoes
nothing visible on either side
lock the door behind me

my Honda is open
driver's door lock broken
have to get to
work   in the pocket
of my jeans is a
quarter
pull it out   a key   shiny
scintillating not an ordinary key
I try to start the
car with it
it is thirty-one
below

iii

The Dissatisfied Customer

you know, after all these years
this GST still pisses me right off
says the man in the chair
just take the sides a bit, Stuey
and I'd love one of your shaves

Stu stops   the man's left
cheek shaven the other
waiting foamed razor
poised in Stu's right hand
his left eye a sudden
flashing crescent
of purple and green
me in a car trapped
inside freezing

hey! where the hell are you going?
the apron dangles
between the man's thighs as he rises
a Rockwell cliché singing aproned unshaven
Lida Rose where the hell are you going?
Stu's back retreats up the stairs
two at a time
sees me frozen in ice
a fallen sculpture in a small back yard

iv

Stu

finds me
fingers frozen

on the passenger seat
a little pile of coins
surely one will start it
he pulls me inside feeds me soup
I eat as if I'm starved
I sweat though I've been in
winter an hour

he peels sticky shirts off me
I hold my arms up, a child
dressing for bed
I speak a language Stu does not

later I learn my brain is swollen
pressure on my skull
has reached my speech centre
I talk and talk
he understands nothing
wraps me in a blanket
guides me to his car
starts it with a key
I remember saying I could not
start my car   my key was
beautiful but it wouldn't work

we drive   I know we are going too fast
I can't keep track my head is rolling
I see a light around his head
he understands nothing
he understands
everything

v

Skull Angels

my doctor leans over me
lights flash in my head
most of his face is obscured
covered by the seraphim in my skull
their wings beat before my eyes

do you know who I am?

you're a doctor
my doctor

do you know my name?

no

do you recognize your husband?

he's sitting over there

do you know his name?

no

I cannot look at him
ashamed I cannot name him
wings thrash at the insides
of my eyelids

vi

My Show, My Show
[for Tim Lilburn]

in my rare waking moments
over the next few days
I say two words in English
my show   my show
I am wheeled into quarantine
repeat the phrase over and over
a melodramatic actor in a Victorian
costume and corset   the back of one hand
pressed to my forehead   fingers
pointing upward

I fall across a divan centred
in a pool of pink
and amber light   sacrifice
myself for my art

the needle enters my spine
the audience jumps to its feet
I stoop to pick up roses

Mom Sleeping

my mother lies on two orange
hospital chairs pulled together
the nurses told her she couldn't
sleep in here   she told them
to fuck off   I wake at four a.m.
my fever has not broken

spinning blades in every
corner flashes of silver
my mom looks cold
though she has a blanket
I am covered with a thin sheet
blinds clink against the glass
carnations and lilies
move in cheerful pink vases
their stems poking into wet green foam
the petals sway   little cards perched in
plastic holders ripple in the false breeze

my mom's hair moves when the air
turns to her   my own hair
full of the wings of thrones

viii

Fresh Fruit Tray

I keep one hand on my fruit
so it cannot fly away
mom is talking to me
showing me pictures of my wedding
two years earlier

I must remember to ask the nurse
for another plate to control the fruit
I will place the second plate
over the first
if the fruit attempts to fly
it will hit the upturned plate

mom asks me if I remember
marrying Stu, he in a blue tux
me in grandma's ivory gown

I will know if the fruit has tried
to escape   I will hear
muffled thumps
see traces of juice
on the upper plate

I take the picture
careful not to release fruit
through the fingers of my other hand
Stu and I stand before friends, my sister
dolled up   beaming
looks like a good time
quite a party

I drop the photo on my lap
mom picks it up
smooths it into the album
wipes her eyes
I need both
hands now to cover the fruit

ix

Mom

Light sometimes passes through me
I am exhausted
my temperature almost normal
though I vomit every hour
and there is too much light
I have tried to chase the bright wings
from my eyes

my mom is reading
something near my bed
her hair is radiant with a crescent halo
half of her face missing
I tell her   she takes
my hand and places it
on the side of her face
I can't see

Rupture

meningitis is the initial diagnosis
before the results come back
everyone must wash their hands
after touching me

my fever and the constant running water
to the left of my head
rupture my inner ear
there is a crumple
of tinfoil when anyone speaks to me

I hear through the distorted
noise of wrinkled steel
there are people in my room always
I am unable to identity them
by sight or sound   now
I see my husband's name

xi

The Hook

The Visiting Director
bends under the yellow tape
he's come to bring me something
a card from the cast and crew
he was sent to hurry me up

I can't see him very well
how did he get into my room?
my eardrum crackles
under his pleading

behind him Mother Courage breaks
the quarantine tape across my
door with her weary body
she hauls her cart into my room singing
of torture the Thirty Years War
time for your medication she says
she lifts an ancient chalice
from a hook on the side of her wagon
you'll have to leave now sir
I drink the Mother's Holy Elixir

xii

Revelation of Divine Love

*... my sight began to fail, and it was all dark about me in the chamber ... save
in the Image of the Cross....All that was away from the Cross was of horror to
me, as if it had been greatly occupied by the fiends.*

Julian of Norwich

I start to see faces
the halos above them
grow fainter

my family looks less like images of the
risen Christ as each day passes
Christ has been here, I'm sure of that
He's been here as He was for Julian

in her mad need for Him
she saw Him hovering
over her   dripping blood and bits
of brain on her nakedness
He shimmering above her
she bleeding her desire

*methought it passed bodily
death, my pains. I thought:
Is any pain like this?*

what they don't tell you
is after the shimmerings dissolve
and before the migraine hits
a half hour of painful lust passes
you'll fuck anything then

and the blood was so plenteous to my sight
that ... if it had been so in kind
and in substance ... it should have made the bed
all one blood

Julian in delirious
ecstasy waits in bed for
the wounds
the naked broken
arms of Jesus

xiii

Coruscans Lux

[after Hildegard of Bingen]

the tilted crescent moon
of the radiant being above
my left eye
His arms bend downward
encircling my skull, the breath
exhaled by bears
goats snakes
propels the scintillating
fortress walls the zigzag
and screech of corners
buttresses angles

O gleaming light of the stars
O bright Jewel!

my hand before my
face a swarm of purplegreen
maggots of light and diamond

O holy breath!
O flame of love!

most will only guess at this splendour
the Godhead quivers just
out of my seeing

Clot of Light

after two weeks
squinting   nauseous
they release me
the sun a clot of light
in my skull rats running
under my scalp

I have apologized to
nurses doctors everyone I could find
for my violence
my raging hands and spit
the vomit and feverish lashing out

the curtains are drawn
my house is too small for these flowers
I'll send some home with mom

Stu welcomes me in
my weightless head
my tender body

he makes soup
he has set a place for me

It Goes on Notwithstanding

I force myself to see it
closing night   as I suspect
it is terrible

the audience hates *Mother Courage*
and stays away in droves
I relish the empty seats
people I know wish me well
comment on the guts it must take
to come back here

house lights fade
the stage goes to black
night falls in the bleeding mountains
I imagine I see Mother Courage backstage
waiting in the wings for her cue
I sit in the dim blue dark
of the audience   the spill from
a booth light casts my shadow on the back
of the man in front of me
a white pool appears at centre
Mother Courage enters   hauls her wagon
stage left   she looks
smaller than I remember
I know how it ends
she's the only one left alive

xvi

The Worst Show I've Ever Seen

my head still bothers me
especially when the acting is this bad
my retinas spin
halos around first-year faces

I need pills to make it through Act Two
just before second intermission I squeeze
Stu's thigh   whisper *I'll be spending*
Act Three in the bar

we pass The Visiting Director in the foyer
the show is starting   better grab your seats

No thanks I answer

~

it's not true what they say
it *will* fall apart if you're not there
I'm living proof
I am indispensable

Awakenings

ever see that movie where Robin Williams
brings Robert De Niro out of his
encephalitic coma with some good drugs
and a tennis ball?

I figure the coma would be great
especially if the first thing I saw when I woke up
was Robert De Niro in one of those
open back gowns
unable to defend himself
against my lucid advances

IV.

Take, eat; this is my body

Matthew 26:26

The Separation of Church and Theatre

[*Godspell* 1989]

do you believe in God?
The Director asks me at
first read-through

That has nothing to do with
how well I'm going to run this show
I reply, annoyed

actors on all sides pipe up
oh yes! cries Karla
Matt is next to testify
of course, Jesus is the Son of God
and He died for our sins

the Son of God will
play a Major Role in this show
preaches The Director pounding his fist
on the ground plans
I want the audience to feel our faith!
I want them to know we believe!

I lean over the table and finalize
my costume fitting schedule
I don't tell them about my nocturnal
visits from The Lord
how the rafters shake with the Love of Jesus!

Day by Day

backstage they whisper and spit
a week before opening
they sway, arms locked
singing *Day by Day*
faces forced into actor smiles
as if I can't tell they
hate one another, as if I can't see
the bile at the corners
of their mouths

I remove my headset
hear raging from the wings stage right
it's Matt and Karla again
the endless brawl about who gets to
play Jesus H. Christ for the most minutes
I switch off my blue-gelled lamp
leave my production table, walk on
stage, exit upstage left
through the loading dock door
the house lights are out
no one sees me leave
when rehearsal stops
dead they notice

I am taking:
Fiorinal for migraines
Gravol for nausea
Elavil for depression
Halcion for insomnia
Tylenol 3 for headaches the Fiorinal won't touch

The Director follows me out
begs me to return
I enter the theatre
his arm around me
he knows it's his power to persuade
I know my pills
are in a bag under my table

For This Is My Body

I fill the Jesus basket
stage left with pita bread so Robin
may feed his disciples

Take, eat;
this is my body

he reaches in
for the second night in a row
the bread is missing
I call backstage
to Bobbie who's reading
Nietzsche between cues
she tells me someone saw
Ryan munching after his big
Thirty Pieces of Silver scene

Ryan's been evicted
I now remember I've seen him
in the student lounge eating
crackers by the dozen
clear and red striped wrappers
littering the floor at his feet

at notes I tell Ryan if he eats
the Jesus food again I'll break his
homeless actor balls

before the Last Supper tonight
I run down to stage left
check Robin's supply
hand it to him from the wings

I stay till it's safely in the
mouths of future saints

Alone with Ryan on Mainstage

I close up at 11:30
post tomorrow's calls
flip the breakers at stage right
turn off the grid lights

as I turn from the panel I feel him
standing at the stage door
I have yet to lock
everyone has left
the commissionaire is on his rounds
which always include
coffee with the security guy half way
across campus

he's blocked my exit
I begin to lose my sight
he would betray me
the first chance he got
he thinks I pick on him
give him the most notes after
rehearsal, always point out
the lines he's missed
the props he eats
I keep telling him to move the damn
microphone away from his mouth
if he wants anyone to understand
what he's singing

he could kill me
I think he wants to
he wants to tell someone I'm not
fit to run this show
I take too many pills
how can I be trusted to call the cues
properly? he's seen me
shoving the blue ones into my mouth
when I think no one is watching

but he says nothing
still sweating from the intensity of the show
blond curls unwashed
stink of old clothes hangs between us
he smiles, then says   *night Kimmy*

he turns to leave, I run to the door
feel for the keyhole, squint past
the twinkling
locking myself in till I think he's
gone to wherever
he sleeps

I know it's in this building
I do not know where

An Opportunity to Betray Him

the role of Judas is demanding
no doubt about it   especially
when you have to play him
in a clown suit and big red
running shoes   a whistle
and a fat cigar

it's too much for Ryan
he disappears half way
through the run, takes
the bag of silver with him
thirty coins won't get him far
but far enough away from me

I'll find a new Judas for week two

On Meeting the Superstar

I am usurped
the touring show stage manager
has taken her position on my
stool in the wings stage right
she wears my headset
but she's moved the microphone
I'll have to completely readjust it

I'm not allowed on stage
the show is self-contained
a full crew of twelve sets up,
strikes, drives to the next town

the front row seats
are some consolation
afterward I hang around the
stage door of my own theatre
like any good disciple

I've been waiting
nearly thirty years to meet him
since my dad took me to see him
on screen in nineteen seventy-three
desert heat and sweat in his hair
his robe ratty at the hem
he crawls up rocks barefoot at dusk
beads swing and dancers
surround him, kick up sand
his friends climb on that bus
at the end of the movie, leave him
hanging there

I elbow my way to the front
he must see me first

he tells me he's played Jesus Christ
twelve hundred and thirty-eight times
and still gets off

he thinks he *is* Jesus
you can tell by the way he holds his
hands always blessing you
all the right Jesus Moves

I fold myself into his robes
at this dark back door
I've met Jesus
and I know this actor
who nuzzles me
is anything but
Christ-like

Where **Does** *She Get Her Courage?*

[A play in One Act for Meah]

Dramatis Personae:
>Mother Courage
>A Woman in Bed
>A Pharmacist

[Hospital Room. Night. Lighting is fluorescent, from the hallway. Inside the room, a Woman in Bed slides on the edge of sleep. There is just enough spill from the hall to illuminate her. There are several machines attached to the Woman. She is fitful and tosses. Mother Courage enters the room from upstage right and crosses downstage centre to a tight amber pool. She is wearing rags, fingerless gloves and pieces of the coats she has scavenged on the battlefield. She looks robust despite her pale skin and the dirt and blood caking her face and hands. She holds up a brown bottle in a gnarled hand and smiles a large toothless grin.]

MOTHER COURAGE [To the audience]: Hi there! I'm Mother Courage. I find that after a long day of pulling this wagon through my ravaged homeland, my natural rhythm can be thrown off by all the war and disease I see around me. You know, it's no easy job hauling all your possessions in a huge cart with a creaky wheel over dead bodies and scarred landscapes, and as a woman, I know it's important to take care of myself. That's why I drink *Mother Courage* Brand Miracle Elixir. When I need a little something to soothe my jangled nerves, *Mother Courage* Brand is just what the doctor ordered.

[Mother Courage rises and floats over the bed to the stage left side and begins adjusting the controls on the I.V. pump. The Woman in Bed continues to toss, not quite awake.]

MOTHER COURAGE [From above the I.V. pump, to the Woman in Bed]: I wanted to be as healthy as I could be, so I talked to my pharmacist.

[A Pharmacist enters the room from upstage right. Her name tag reads *Jenn*. She has long red hair, she is wearing glasses and a white lab coat, and is holding a thick blue folder with the words *CLINICAL STUDY* printed on it in enormous letters.]

PHARMACIST: Clinical studies have shown that 9 out of 10 patients who regularly used *Mother Courage* Brand Miracle Elixir showed marked improvement in motor coordination and stamina on long hauls through their war-torn neighbourhoods. 8 out of 10 patients found that they were now able to look at dead bodies with no serious side effects other than dry mouth, nausea, vomiting, severe rash, intravenous drug allergies, fever, swelling of the brain, excessive weeping, delirium, hallucinations, visions of God, constipation, and occasional sleeplessness. [She vanishes.]

MOTHER COURAGE [To the Woman in Bed]: Since I began using *Mother Courage* Brand Miracle Elixir every day, my skin is softer, I have more energy, and I've lost 10 pounds! Try it on its own, or with Gravol, Penicillin, Demarol, Halcion and a nice Morphine drip. It'll get you back on your feet and you'll be ready to face that wagon another day, the shadow of poverty and disease a distant memory. [To the audience] Look for it hanging from the sides of fine wagons everywhere.

[Mother Courage hovers above the I.V. drip, liquefies and enters the I.V. tube, a thin strip of blue pulsing into the arm of the Woman in Bed. The brown bottle clinks to the floor and rolls under the radiator. Blackout. Curtain.]

V.

Oliver!

Opening Night, Mainstage

The Designer roars at me
says he needs to touch
up the stage
actor shoes have scuffed
the pattern here and here
the house opens in fifteen minutes
he stumbles   kneels heavily
begins slopping paint on stairs stage right
covering the glow tape I've placed there warning
of edges in darkness
the edges of their skirts hiding
their feet   floating

I've seen this show before
calm   I tell him I must open the house
he flails the brush at me
drops of grey hit my cheek
I wouldn't understand, he reminds me
I'm just the stage manager I wouldn't
understand the artistic needs
of the show how actors destroy
the work he's done
trash it like graffiti kids
on a new painted wall

I must get him out
steady the paint bucket, its contents
precariously balanced downstage right
coax the brush free from
a palm greystained and sweating

The Designer is reeling
howling blame at me
through a locked door
for footprints and scuffs as though
I were responsible for actors having to touch
the ground when they walk

We Get this Same Old Gruel

twelve boys under the age of thirteen
thank you Christ
I never have to see them
until the Overture   through glass
Stu takes care of them before the show
smacks his Fagan stick on the floor of Studio A
to shut them the hell up

they stumble on cute as can be
twelve barefoot orphans dreaming
of food glorious food in an
evil underworld of orphan-starving madmen
every night at least one of them isn't onstage
please get somebody, I don't care who I tell Stu
fill in Jonah's spot, it's past his bedtime

they barely make it through
curtain call standing
they're so tired poor darlings
holding those bowls out
singing the wrong words
off-key night after night
living to drive me mad

this tinted window separates me
from the carnage that is Act One
an unwilling parent squinting
through maternity glass
at an unwanted child
my booth is a hundred feet away across
a dark expanse of mom and dad heads
paid good money to see their
angels perform

Stage Mother

[for Les]

Jonah's mother says she must stand
in the wings stage right
every performance to coach him
on the words to *Got to Pick a Pocket or Two*
remind him how to smile

my most devoted parent volunteer
she's here every night to do their
make-up for them, tousle their hair,
lead them in vocal exercises
if you boys could just listen to Jonah
he's got that scale exactly right
Jonah, you show them how it's done

I feel for poor Jonah but I still
can't stand the little bastard

Jonah's dad came for one
rehearsal to help with the boys
and never came back
flinching, embarrassed by her thin
fingers tugging at their son's
costume and laces
he left the theatre and got into their van
can't blame him
I wish I *were* him   at home
on the couch watching some tube

as it is, I have a show to do and
stage mothers everywhere
each wearing too much perfume
filling the wings, waving to get her
boy's attention
Bill Sikes and his dog try to
get by a pack of mothers planted
between two flats downstage right
it's their cue but
they can't get on stage
a silhouetted flock of pantomiming
women with big hair and bigger
mouths are blocking their path

after the first week, I take action
re-block Jonah to stand upstage left
behind the other boys in the number
it's because he's taller
I explain to his mother, one hand
to my cheek wiping away her
furious spittle
I've moved the shorter boys downstage
for sight lines

no matter where she stands
she cannot see him
he is buried

I hang a sign on the back door
NO PARENTS PERMITTED ON STAGE

these are the mothers
hungry Dickensian boys
ran away from
their preening and preaching
and blending pancake make-up
on tired little cheeks that don't
care anymore   from the wings
in front of all the other kids
—their faces covered in a thick
veneer of make-up—
they mouth the lines they never
got to say

Consider Yourself

it must be that corset
laced up too tight or too many
generations of dancers
wearing those sweaty tap shoes
I see how that could be annoying

it's the finale
the god damn curtain call
the audience is on its feet
mom and dad roses pelt
my bowing weeping actors

But my character was sexually
abused as a child
she tells me at notes that night
when I ask her to explain the forced smile
the weep-for-me pout during the only
happy number in the show

it's the curtain call
I remind her gently   *it's* Oliver!
everyone's clapping for you
we're not doing Hamlet
you are not the tragic Ophelia
you're the third peasant girl from the left
get out there and dance and smile
I don't care if your CHARACTER
was run over by a train
smile for Christ Sakes!

Saturday night, her beaming teeth
are pointed directly at me
her shoes are too tight
her corset strangles her
I hum along smiling back

Program Note from The Director

Merry Christmas! For your Yuletide family enjoyment the Theatre Studies Program is proud to present **Oliver!** *It's a heartwarming musical tale of a dirty, starving orphan boy living in the gutters and alleys of mid-nineteenth century London.*

You know the words! Sing along as he escapes the horrors of the orphanage. Follow his adventures as a gang of thugs befriends him, teaches him to steal, shows him the intricacies of violence and the joys of greed.

We hope you've brought the kids, because the highlight of this festive show will come halfway through Act Two when Bill Sikes, in a fit of jealousy, bludgeons his girlfriend Nancy to death on stage. The actor playing Sikes gives his best performance yet as Sikes becomes more and more violent and aroused as the beating continues. It's all part of our Christmas gift to you, the audience. Enjoy!

There will be one twenty-minute intermission.

The Director

The *Why I Quit My Job* Poem

I see the flames first
the result of The Misguided
Director's belief that this show needed
fireworks
it's Christmas after all

I call the house lights up
send Bobbie on with the extinguisher
a technician flies in the burning curtain
      applause
the same crowd that claps when
a waiter drops a tray full of glass and food
in a few moments the show goes on
burnt fire retardant stink fogging the keylights

the fire has caused a short in the headsets
I have no cues for a few minutes
and the actors will need placating
I'm on my way to the stage
but the booth's doorknob comes
off in my hand
I'm locked in a film noir nightmare

can't talk to anyone, I have no idea
what's going on down there
the sides of my head cave in
my crew takes their cues on their own
I send the sound man out
over the heads of the audience
he clanks up the spiral staircase
from the booth to the catwalk
a maze of blue metal suspended
high over the crowd
he tries not to drop coins and dirt
into laps and open programs fifty feet below
climbs down the ladder from the flies stage right
finds a commissionaire with keys

now my show sound has cut out too
the dialogue on stage muffled
through thick glass
the sound of every adult in
a Charlie Brown cartoon
actors glance up to the booth between lines
they see me in dim blue trying
to open the door

VI.

...seek the deepness

The Dead One Lying Before You

cheap Chilean white wine
drink it digging hunks of cheese,
mushrooms, strips of lettuce out of
salad that never makes it
to our plates
Dawn, we drink and whine about Thursdays
our worst classes
me dreaming through *Eighteenth Century Literature
and the Law* reading *Bleak House* as
some kind of distorted
family law document
you in your *Gross Anatomy 1* class
carve at dead bodies, peel back
skin, dissect muscle
you nearly pass out the first day
some kids do, the formaldehyde
stench is too much

you spend an afternoon dissecting
cheek muscles of a girl
your own age
no one should have to do that, you say
you want to know do people come back
after they die
I tell you yes

imagine you a year later on that cold slab
masked Physio first-years at you with
scalpels and gauze
what do they talk about while they
dissect you?
that great party they went to last night?
how the formaldehyde in their
fermented veins and the waft of it
from bodies combine
in nauseous waves? do they work quietly

with respect the way you always did
speaking only of the dead one lying before you
showing her the greatest reverence possible
slicing?

I have a glass of wine
take a bike ride the moment
I hear your head has hit
the side window on a deserted grid road
ride through late April cool   six at night
no words of you
breeze helping me breathe, wind
and sunset in my hair

Scene 20
[for Karen and Larry]

Dramatis Personae:
>A Former Stage Manager
>Larry, her brother
>Dawn, her niece

[February. The lighting is indoor, late evening. In an upstage corner of the living room, a Rubbermaid Stor-All is tucked away. Inside are skeleton parts. The clear plastic box is marked REHAB 282: *Gross Anatomy 1*. This room is strewn with clean human bones and bits of the Former Stage Manager's unfinished paper on postcolonial Nigerian fiction. From the CD player in the living room stage left, we hear David Wilcox singing "The Rainy Night Saloon." Larry sits stage right at the dining room table. He is tall, handsome, laid back. He fiddles with the tab on his can of Pepsi. The Former Stage Manager sits stage left, picking apple slices from the wooden salad bowl at the centre of the table. In front of her is an empty glass of Chilean white wine. The Former Stage Manager's niece is at a Physiotherapy pajama party tonight.]

LARRY: You want some more salad?

THE FORMER STAGE MANAGER [Reaching into the salad bowl and grabbing a huge handful of lettuce and cheese]: Nope, I'm good.

LARRY: Okay. [Pause.] How about some wine? I'm going to get another Pepsi. [She nods her head yeah. He rises, picks up her glass, and crosses downstage right to the small fridge. The lights intensify slightly in this area as his next line is delivered from the refrigerator.] So why did you quit your theatre job? [Larry pours the wine for her, replaces the bottle in the fridge and crosses to the dining room table.]

THE FORMER STAGE MANAGER: Thanks. I started dreaming about Macbeth. I was having visions of Macbeth. Not normal. [She chuckles to herself.] I had to get out of there.

[Dawn enters the room from upstage left. She is tall, beautiful and dressed in pajamas.]

DAWN: Hi you guys! How was dinner?

LARRY: Great. How was your thing?

DAWN: It sucked, but thanks for asking. [She tosses her keys on the kitchen table, reaches into the salad bowl, digs till she finds a couple of radishes and stuffs them into her mouth. She crosses stage left, chewing noisily. She lands on the loveseat in the living room and peels off her snow-covered slippers. She fires them, one after the other, toward the orange cat who sits in the foyer among the boots downstage left.]

THE FORMER STAGE MANAGER: You want some salad?

DAWN: Nope I'm good. I'm going to bed. See you in the morning. [She thunders up the stairs two at a time and falls into bed, already dressed for it.]

LARRY: You were saying about the visions.

THE FORMER STAGE MANAGER: Something is going to happen to her. Something is going to happen to her.

LARRY: No it isn't.

THE FORMER STAGE MANAGER: Yes it is.

LARRY: Nothing's going to happen.

THE FORMER STAGE MANAGER: I had to leave, Larry. I was dreaming about Macbeth, for Christ sakes.

LARRY: I gotta go to bed. [He puts his Pepsi can on the table, rises, crosses downstage and kisses his sister on the forehead. It's her night for dishes. He crosses stage right and climbs the stairs slowly. He is half way up the stairs for the next line.]

THE FORMER STAGE MANAGER: Me too. Night.

[The Former Stage Manager begins to collect plates but changes her mind. She sinks to the ground, the plates piled on the table. She lies down and nods off. She sleeps on the area rug under the dining room table. This is her dream: A man is bloodied. He walks in blood. In the dream are wild animals. She runs with animals and rips the arms and legs from corpses in the night, chewing on them.]

The stars have hidden
their fires
Light sees not her black
and deep desires

[Fade to black. Curtain.]

Nieces

I named you *Barnacle Sue*
loved to watch you over the edge
as you clung to the side
of the boat, wanting to be in the water
but close to me at the same time
life jacket bashing your chin
with each slap of water against the side

~

I love that I can share a glass
of wine with you now, Tricia
your hair of old gold tied back
we sip a cool Pinot in a
Saskatoon bar
you tell me about the
hot guy you met
at the university mixer last weekend
I don't tell you to be careful

~

Jennifer
freckles and lip,
unruly mass of orange-red hair
your apartment a riot of text books
big sister's furniture
you're damn cool but not too cool
to hug your auntie
usually just after your ten kilometre run
you rub a sweaty
cheek against mine

~

there's a hungover
Sunday school teacher on my couch
in men's pajama bottoms, grey tank top
Dawn, half asleep, moaning through
bleary-eyed morning
untouched glass of grapefruit juice
on the coffee table
you awaken   ask if I'll make pancakes
smile at me, promise to do dishes
you switch on cartoons

~

my nieces and I cruise for guys
in my new car
I drive, they take turns
reaching through the open sunroof
waving and screeching at good-looking boys
switch seats so they can all
have a turn in front with me
the other three squashed in the back
elbow each other, laughing
parents left behind
rain falls through the hole in the roof
we lift our faces to the coolness

Scene 21

[Setting: Rural Saskatchewan. Location may be indicated by wind, dust and wheat just planted. Lighting is outdoor, early afternoon. Leafy gobos. Dawn and a friend leave Dawn's mother's house and get into the friend's car, which consists of two black folding chairs at centre. Dawn sits downstage in the passenger seat. The friend is driving. The car doors and steering wheel are mimed. We hear the sound of a car starting. The sound should come from a speaker placed near the chairs. The car accelerates. The actor playing the friend should make gestures toward driving, without being distracting. The two come to a stop sign on a gravel-covered grid road. An oil tanker crosses in front of them. The friend does not see the truck behind it and pulls into the intersection. As the two vehicles collide, the friend is thrown from the car in slow motion. Dawn is tossed against the passenger side window, also in slow motion. Her head hits the glass with great force. The actors should take care that their slow motion acting appear natural and not exaggerated. Light fades at centre.]

One More Wintering

… seek the deepness and water the plants in time.

Julian of Norwich

a time will come when I can once again
drink Santa Rita Chardonnay
a time when I may eat
a radish without tears
I remember your Volkswagen-shaped
slippers, your homemade Hawaiian pizza,
bones all over our
living room floor
we were always tripping on stray
femurs, the metacarpals and phalanges
in a heap under the CD rack

~

I cannot keep this rose alive
the third one I've planted for you
Persian Yellow is hearty
grows everywhere downtown
crews of orange-vested teenagers
cut them back each week
you can't see past the flowers
at intersections, branches reach
scrape at hoods and driver's doors
cadmium yellow petals in the wipers
yet in my back yard
it will not take hold

I planted it in the corner of the garden
a week after your death so I could
look out on it as I wrote

but I don't write
I watch it month after month
watch it overcome by
black spot, pear slugs, not enough
sun, too much sun, maybe the verbena
crowds it, maybe it wants
less water
more water
maybe I need to dig it up
clean earth from roots
lay the plant on the soil
let it moisten and shrink
under winter snow
let its decay nourish the dusty miller,
violas, dianthus

~

one more wintering
I'll sit inside with a tall glass of chilled wine
watch the barren branches
poking up through snow
they say it might live
if I don't cut it back till spring
if I add a scoop of bone
meal to the dirt, maybe it will awaken

next August, I'll bend to pull
radishes fresh from soil, snap the
tops, crunch red bulbs, sip my wine

VII.
Then comes my fit again:
A Dream in Two Acts

Firefighters in Smoky Stage Debut!

[The Scottish Play]

An actor walked on stage and yelled, "Macbeth!" into the empty theatre. At that moment, a stage light ignited one of the curtains. The Stage Manager was treated in hospital for smoke inhalation and released.

The Sun

one must never say *Macbeth*
inside the theatre
unless one is actually rehearsing
or performing that play or reciting
actual lines in which the name
Macbeth actually appears
for certain death
shall surely befall one who utters
the cursèd word under any other circumstances

if the *M Word* is spoken within theatre walls
the offending actor/technician must leave the
immediate area via the nearest exit
the guilty party must stand outside the door
turn three times
spit   swear (*Pisspots* is good)   knock
be granted permission to enter
promise never to do it again

Oh, yes, there's something going on,
The Director says to the reporter
But every production is magic in some way.
You just have to get it working for you.

and get it working for him he does!
on my way up to the catwalk above the stage
to heroically show the firefighters
where the escape hatch leads to the roof
the smoke fills me
my second trip to the hospital
(oxygen masks thin blankets
running nurses eye drops)
doesn't dampen his theatrical spirit one bit

Stage Management Pre-show Checklist—*Macbeth*

6:45 pm

-Open stage doors
-Open dressing rooms
-Work lights onstage and in house
-Actor call

7:00 pm

-Check actor sign-in sheet
-Tech call
-Ropes tied off upstage left, upstage centre, downstage right
-Sweep and Coke-mop wings and platforms
-Imagine spending entire evening with husband some day
-Yeah. Right.

7:10 pm

-Macbeth harness check
-Sword Fights and Murders run-through
-Lights—replace all Act One gels

7:20 pm

-Full cast warm-up
-Curtain call run-through
-Notes
-Blood prep
-You promised yourself never to get this tired again

7:30 pm

-Clear stage
-Half-hour call
-Set all banquet stools in wings stage right
-Platform stage right to yellow spikes
-Turn downstage legs to face up-down

-Tape backstage doors open
-Fill water jugs
-Settle actor fight in Dressing Room C
-Warm up fog machines
-Macbeth's sword and gloves stage right
-Witches' mics on
-Check candles
-Remind Brian (for the 49th time) that it's MACbeth, not
        MICbeth
-Charge glow tape

-Safety Check
        *secure ground cloth
        *platform brakes on
        *blue lights backstage on
        *glow tape blackout check
        *wings and crossover clear
        *stash Kaluha Mudslides under SM desk
        *trap door secure
        *trap room blue lights on
        *check sword and dagger hilts

7:40 pm

-Preset lights (Q 0.5)
-Work lights and booth lights out
-Preset witches under drop cloth
-Sympathize with 19-year-old first-year baby girl under drop
        cloth claiming fabric allergies and sore muscles from
        crouching under there for twenty minutes
-Pretend to care
-Start soundQ 0.3 and deck fog machine
-Chase The Designer off the deck

7:45 pm

–Open the house
–15 minutes and house open call

7:55 pm

–5 minute call
–Act One beginners (Macbeth, Banquo, Bloody Sergeant,
        Duncan) to the stage
–Crew to headset
–Look out over the heads of your audience

7:58 pm

–Try to remember why you loved it
–Stand by

At House Open, SoundQ 0.3 and Deck Fog Running

8:01—Go
Standby House Lights, LightQ 0.6, 1, 2, 3, and Q5
Standby Trap Fog
Actors stand by
Standby SoundQ 0.4 and 0.5
House Lights to half Go
House Lights out and LightQ 0.6 Go
Trap Fog Go
SoundQ 0.4 Go
LightQ1 Go

Act One, Scene One
FIRST WITCH: *When shall we three meet again?*

LightQ 2 Go
  SECOND WITCH: *In thunder, lightning or in rain?*

LightQ 3 Go
Trap Fog out Go
Standby Deck Fog out
  THIRD WITCH: *When the hurlyburly's done,*
        When the battle's lost and won.

LightQ 5 Go
  SECOND WITCH: *That will be ere set of sun.*

Standby SoundQ 0.6, 0.7, 1 and 1.1
  FIRST WITCH: *Where the place?*
  THIRD WITCH: *Upon the heath.*

Standby LightQ 6, 7 and 8
  SECOND WITCH: *There to meet with*
  ALL: *Macbeth.*

SoundQ 0.6 Go
> **FIRST WITCH:** *I come, Graymalkin.*
> **SECOND WITCH:** *Paddock calls.*
> **THIRD WITCH:** *Anon.*
> **ALL:** *Fair is foul and foul is fair.*
> > *Hover through the fog and filthy air.*

LightQ 6 and SoundQ 0.7 Go
SoundQ 1 Go
Deck Fog out Go
> *EXEUNT*
> > **Act One, Scene Two**
Macbeth and Banquo Go

Proverbs★

i

Take pity upon the actors, for they are as children
and must be led with lovingkindness.

my poor babies

it's rough out there
being a Weyard Sister
hunched under a
drop cloth half the show
part of the set, really
only three scenes
I understand

Macbeth tripping on your
ass, your head, whatever
part of you is facing upstage right
when he enters so deep in character
he can't see you
cannot remember you're there
forgets he shouldn't
kick you

the nightly battles rage at notes
witches summoning spirits
threatening to place thumbtacks
banana peels *Keep off the Grass* signs
around your unholy lair

★*borrowed from* The Technician's Bible, *source unknown*

98

I will drain him dry as hay:
Sleep shall neither night nor day
Hang upon his penthouse lid;
He shall live a man forbid

I personally think
your tears only add to the effect
your hideous make-up and rubber pilot's thumb
wrack'd as homeward he did come
its detached tendons hanging
baby heads on sticks
you got the best props

the crying is working for you
I say, oblivious to your pain
go with that

ii

*Give not unto the actors their props before their
time, for as surely as the sun doth rise in the
east they shall lose or break them.*

there are more scabbards in this show
than in the fray at Forres
more swords
than in the entire battle at Dunsinane

thank Christ we didn't stage Birnam Wood
trundling up the hill to the palace
someone could lose an eye

*Let every soldier hew him down a bough,
And bear't before him*

I'd have loved to have seen that—
a bunch of pimply first-years thrust
onto this vast stage carrying poplar branches
cut at night from the park
behind the college
tripping all over each other
falling into the orchestra pit

a blond nineteen-year-old boy
—lost in fantasies of the girls' dressing
room right next to his
waiting for that good cool
beer in the student lounge
in less than an hour, hot
leather chafing the skin of
his inner thighs—
gets to say one line
he positions himself in the light's
hot spot and for all he's worth, he cries
It shall be done!

tonight   just as surely
as Great Birnam Wood
to high Dunsinane Hill shall
come against Macbeth,
on his way to storm the castle
this actor will miss his scabbard
and stab himself in the thigh
with a dull sword

iii

Keep holy the first performance, for afterward,
thou shalt party.

it isn't comfortable but
it is flat and dark
I tell my crew I'm going to catch
a quick nap in the wings stage right
before the Friday matinée
I filch Macbeth's sweaty fake
fur vest from the quick-change rack
use it as a pillow

I lie down between the second and
third legs   drift off
last night's honey wine
hurlyburlying in my skull
I dream of combat and blood

I wake half an hour later
find myself surrounded
by sawhorses and yellow
POLICE LINE DO NOT CROSS tape
I panic   think I am in the
hospital under quarantine
around my body is
a masking tape outline
they marked me where I fell
I stagger to my feet
run my show

the outline remains till
closing night

iv

*Beware of actors during scene changes, for they are
not like unto thee and are blind in the dark.*

most are likely hungover
especially for matinées

this morning my To-Do list reads
Glow-tape the shit out of
every god damn thing

I realize it's hard to see clearly
staring into the front-of-house lights
emoting and spitting
imagining the awed gasps
the audience staggering under
the luminous greatness
of your performance   poor old Shakespeare
unrecognizable on your eighteen
-year-old tongue

in the dark tonight
my stage is a landing strip
and still Lady Macbeth
trips on her costume her candle
extinguished the audience gasps
a floomp of fabric and
expelled air

Act Two

light

blood

dagger

wax

green spotlight

finger of birth-strangl'd babe ditch-deliver'd by a drab

coffee

red keylight

scabbard

crow making wing to the rooky wood

actor

body

witches

wind

black

curtain

The Drugs

the Elavil makes me see double
makes me doubt my flesh still hangs
from my bones

I'm sure it's the drugs
they make me walk out
of rehearsal   cry
at the drop of a hat
scream at my actors
dream of broadswords
the glint of smoky sun
on clanging blades held high
bodies falling before me
either side of me   I carve
my path through them

the drugs make me want
blood make me fill my
mouth with the filthy words
of witches   they make me taste
the cherry of fake blood
I stand at centre stage   take more
than my dosage   the drugs
spill out of my fingers
onto the stage   I fall to my knees clawing
the drop cloth picking up blue pills
what hands are here? ha!
they pluck out mine eyes

I fall onto my back
the catwalk swirls above me
Amber and Nile Blue pierce
my retinas   I sleep

till from my bones my flesh be hack'd

[for Chris Postle]

i

thick my blood

the battle excites him
ripped flesh of foes his sword
through muscle and skin
the king's sweaty embrace
afterward

let him come to my bed
soaked and reeking paw
me with red and crusting
hands leave flakes of other men's
skin on my thighs my lips
the guards' tankards clanking
in the hall outside

when he lays with me I am
an unlucky soldier unable
to draw my sword in time
unseam'd from the nave to the chops
my arms to the sky
armour clanking against my breasts
the blood soaked air
my juices spilling over
the dead near me   my womb billowing
the wound pregnant with the ghosts
of children I will not give him

ii

in blood stepp'd in so far

my arms are thick with it
my secret murders sticking on my hands
I am in the centre of a pool
my head raised
blood lapping my earlobes and chin
the shore is far off
I must go forward through my
sea of sanguine bile

the sea is awash with baby heads
floating apparitions of
children   three women
pronounce me dead

when I drop under
the blood enters my mouth
my tongue thick with it
she throws our son's body
into the sea

I breathe blood
I am King

iii

blood will have blood

more orange than red
it burns vermilion
in the sick yellow light
we cast upon it

it tastes of cherries poured
into blood capsules
when the broadsword enters the belly
the actor bites down
blood trickles from lips

Frank's hands dipped
in a green basin in the wings
stage left   plastic
coats the floor beneath
the blood table
he enters dripping

Will all great Neptune's ocean wash this blood
Clean from my hand?

The Prince of Cumberland dons the dead
tyrant king's crown
stitched into the leather
are tiny sponges soaked with blood
they press against Colin's head
the sweet syrup courses down his
face he catches a drop on
his tongue   the cistern of his lust
runneth over

iv

the taste of it

under pinging halogen I wait
for my cue, my moment
I am poised on a platform at centre
soon, all eyes on me

smear the blood across my lip
I have been in battle
rumple my leather
vest   wait
for the light

a hum signals me, I turn
my face to the burning
lamp from the second LX
a burnt pink washes me

I would the friends we miss were safe arrived

Alan will crown me as he
does every night
he will push the leather round
over my head and say *Hail
King! for so thou art*

he will squeeze the sides just enough
to make the red stickiness
leak down my face
I am King
I taste the blood falling into my mouth
the cherry of it fills me
pink and amber fade
I am King

v

take my milk for gall

we had a child once
I killed it

~

in the stone and dank of
my palace life the wife
of the Thane of Glamis
I nurse it
he in battle
he across oceans   years
returned one fall and
fathered it   fathered the thing
and left again
left for a year into a grey
and thorny fog   his ship tossing

birth tore me end to end
I swore I would not
bear another child
I lay in blood   pushed
the greasy mass from my belly
and dreamed him killing, embracing men
plunging his hands into the warmth of
open bellies on the battlefield
to keep his fingers alive
broadswords enter steaming flesh
last breaths expelled from dying soldiers

a baby suckles me

the fire blazes
my breasts cold in the air its eyes
the eyes of its father
born to that life   battles ruin cruelty
I wrote to him
he could not wait to see his son
told he would not be king
loved him anyway unseen

~

my wench retires
I nurse in the great room
the fire with me always
I have light by me continually
'tis my command

when my love returns
triumphant no doubt
he will find he has no son
the child buried by morning
my lord will be dispatched again
immediately by the king he serves
the weak bloated king

a baby suckles me
my left nipple
encircled by little lips
my left hand
supports a spongy head
kiss sleeping eyelids

grasp the baby's legs with my
right hand and pluck my nipple from
its boneless gums
it opens its eyes
I stand   swing the baby high
over my head
and with the strength I knew I had
I bring its head
down on the edge of the
hearth nine times

the brain falls in chunks
blood spatters walls and floor
I dash the brains out until
the head is gone
a baby dangles
dripping on stones

sleep
I dream battles

vi

till from my bones my flesh be hack'd

applause

I call the house lights up
the audience leaves
programs under chairs
a man in a white dress shirt stands,
stretches, turns to a
friend in the row behind him
looks up hearing Gord's boots
clang along the catwalks
pulling Act Two gels
sliding in sick yellows and greens
for Act One tomorrow afternoon

downstairs, actors wipe
cold cream from tired faces
bitch about corsets, blood packs
the Thane who can't remember his
fucking lines
remove my headset, close my script
push the intercom button on my microphone
my voice floats over their dressing
room speakers
good show   get some sleep
your call is 11:30   curtain at one

crawl down
the ladder from the booth
into the house, Gord above me
singing something from *Ghost*
in the Machine by The Police
as he moves, a dust trail falls from the catwalk
settles on the arms of blue chairs
I walk down wide, orange carpeted stairs
climb on stage and enter

the wings stage left
the blood table is clean
lids replaced daggers waiting
to be bloodied tomorrow
a candlestick sits for a crazy woman
I peel the evening's
wax from its brass
replace it in its masking tape square
Lady M's candle
Gord calls a good night, leaves
through the loading dock doors

here's the smell of the blood still
I cross to centre stage
Frank finds me standing
upstage centre
not moving facing the dark seats
a cross breeze from the open shop doors
moves my hair slightly
he's showered, moist and weary
from his second encounter
with the witches   (he is harnessed,
flown   crucified he swings above them
          the apparitions come)

now   he holds me to him
over his right shoulder a dead
baby floats, I shut
my eyes against its shimmer
kiss my Macbeth
his boots echo in the empty
house   I am alone

stage right
check the witches' props

1] cauldron (items below stored within)
2] an armed child
3] a bloody child (dead)
4] a crowned child (dead)
5] finger of birth-strangl'd babe
6] a pilot's thumb
7] poisoned entrails
8] gruel thick and slab

wash the filthy
witness from my hands

the sword table is neat
blades lined up facing away from the stage
a stray scabbard has fallen
pick up Frank's dagger
I am for the air
rise into the fly tower between
pipes lined with lights
borders curtains masking
Frank's weapon light in my hand
I hack at fabric spinning
clang my blade against
swinging pipes

I see the stage below—
my markings
worn black wood, trap
-doors and dust
hold the blade at arm's length
run my body through, release
the handle, watch the blood fall
to the floor

settle gently into my drop
touch down
pull the blade from my breast
lay it next to a splash of blood
now the charm is firm and good

pull the ghost lamp from the wings downstage left
throw its thin light across the house

Fade. Curtain.

Exeunt Omnes

FINIS

Acknowledgements

deepest thanks to my husband, Stu.

many thanks to Dennis Cooley, to everyone at Turnstone, and to the late Manuela Dias. to Tim Lilburn: thank you for sending me into the woods with old books and older spirits.

thanks to *Sage Hill Writing Experience,* the members of the Fall 2000 Poetry Colloquium, and to Steven Ross Smith. thanks also to the *Saskatchewan Writers Guild* Writers/Artists Colonies.

thanks to Bert Almon, Holly Borgerson Calder, Rebecca Campbell, Ernie Coombs, Olga Costopolous, Joan Crate, David Elias, Lee Elliott, Heidi Greco, Leslie Greentree, Catherine Greenwood, Shawna Lemay, Iman Mersal, April Miller, Sandy Moser, Blaine Newton, Michael Penny, Liz Philips and Larry Reese for careful reading of many of these poems in early stages.

thanks to Father Martin for his blessings, and to Father Demetrius and his mom, the late Elsa Wasylyniuk. many thanks, as always, to St. Peter's Abbey. thank you, Magic Post Office.

thanks to my former colleagues in the Theatre Studies Program, Red Deer College. love and thanks to my families and friends, especially to Karen, Larry, Jalesa and Griffin.

several of these poems have appeared, in slightly different form, in *The Antigonish Review, blue moon, grain, The Prairie Journal of Canadian Literature,* and *Room of One's Own.*

★lines in italics in "Revelation of Divine Love" are from: Juliana of Norwich, *Revelations of Divine Love.*

★lines in italics in "Coruscans Lux" are from: Hildegard of Bingen, *Book of Divine Works.*

★for the Macbeth poems, I used *Allyn and Bacon Academy Series: Macbeth*. Samuel Thurber, ed. Boston: Norwood Press, 1896.